Bay View Academy
Charter School
222 Casa Verde Way
Monterey, CA 93940

BIRTH OF A FOREST

*The author wishes to thank Dr. S. Charles Kendeigh,
Professor of Zoology, University of Illinois, for
reading the manuscript of this book.*

BIRTH OF A FOREST
Text copyright © 1964 by Millicent E. Selsam
Pictures copyright © 1964 by Barbara Wolff
Printed in the United States of America. All rights reserved.

Library of Congress catalog card number: 63-17281

1 89609
5 mar 87

Birth of a Forest

by MILLICENT E. SELSAM

*Illustrated with pictures
by Barbara Wolff
and with photographs*

HARPER & ROW, PUBLISHERS
NEW YORK, EVANSTON, AND LONDON

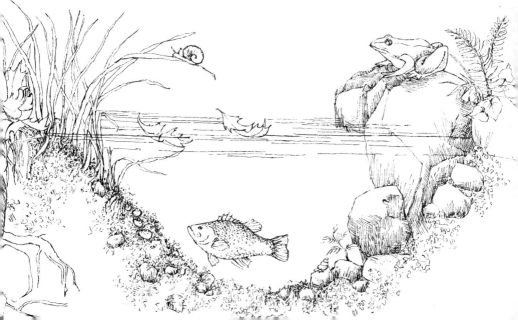

Every part of the earth changes from moment to moment. Day in and day out, year in and year out, the action of wind and rain and sun cracks rocks and wears away mountains. Rivers cut away the soil at their banks and carry it along to where the current is slow. There the soil is dropped and the riverbed slowly fills. On beaches the wind picks up sand and piles it in sand dunes at the back of the beach. At another time, on the same beach, the ocean crashes in and carries much of the sand away.

The same kinds of natural forces slowly but surely fill in lakes. Soil washes in, plants and animals die in the lake, and gradually the lake becomes shallower and shallower until it changes to dry land on which prairie grasses or tall forest trees may grow. No one person could possibly see this happen. It may take hundreds or even thousands of years for an area once covered by a lake to become a prairie or a forest. Yet we know that such changes do take place. Scientists have found ways of learning about these changes that have gone on in the past. They have found the clues to the story in places where there are a series of lakes, some of which are known to be much older than others.

USDA PHOTO

This was the case near Lake Michigan. Once the level of this lake was much higher than it is today. As the water level fell and the lake retreated what was once the bottom of the lake became dry land. The land was not level but in the form of ridges with hollows between. Water was left in these hollows and rain water collected in them. A new series of small lakes or ponds were formed. All this took place very slowly, so that the oldest ponds were farthest away from the shores of Lake Michigan and the youngest ones were very close to its shores. By studying these ponds of different ages, scientists

Series of ponds

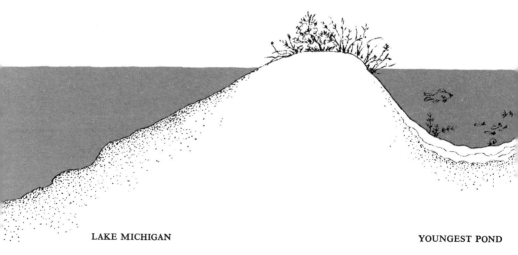

LAKE MICHIGAN   YOUNGEST POND

worked out the story from pond to forest. They studied many other ponds and lakes as well and discovered the same kind of story. Most small lakes eventually disappear and become part of the land. Very large and very deep lakes change too, but much more slowly.

Our story begins with a new pond just formed near Lake Michigan. It is a particular story, but it shows the general way ponds in other places may change. As the story unfolds, different kinds of plants and animals enter the pond and replace the ones that were there before. Where do they all come from?

OLDER PONDS

Animals always produce a great number of offspring that move into new areas, sometimes by accident and sometimes in their search for food. If they happen to reach an area suitable for them, they remain. But how do they reach new ponds?

Some animals fly or are light enough to be carried by the wind. Some, like turtles, frogs, salamanders, and snakes, can creep, run, or hop over land. Some, like fish, swim to a pond through channels or streams that connect it to other bodies of fresh water. The same channels may bring eggs of many animals as well as the animals themselves. Worms, clams, snails, and insects might not get to a pond by swimming, but they are light enough to be carried by the water. When birds such as ducks, rails, and herons fly to new bodies of water, they often have tiny animals or the eggs of larger animals stuck in the mud on their feet.

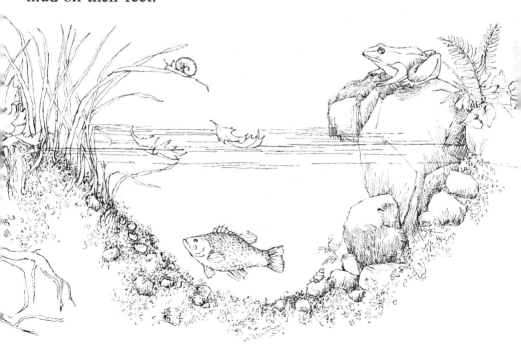

Although most plants cannot move by themselves from one place to another, they do get to new areas all the same. Bits and pieces of simple water plants called *algae* float into a pond and grow into whole new plants. The wind brings many seeds. Some seeds, such as those of the maple, ash, and elm, have winged extensions. The wings make the seeds whirl in the air and delay their fall to the ground. As long as they are in the air, the wind picks them up and carries them farther along. Other seeds have hairy plumes like little parachutes that help them stay up in the air for long periods. Some seeds are so light that they can just float in the air.

Water birds carry seeds on their bills, feet, and feathers. If you have ever dipped your hand into water that has many seeds floating on it, you know how they cling when you lift your hand out of the water. In the same way seeds cling to the feathers and feet of birds.

Many birds eat fruits. The juicy parts are digested and the seeds pass through the birds' digestive tracts. The birds may eat these fruits near one pond and then fly to another pond, where the seeds are deposited in their droppings. Over twelve hundred water lily seeds were found in the stomach of one duck! Most seeds are not harmed by their passage through the birds' digestive tracts. Some sprout more easily because their hard seed coats are softened by the digestive juices.

Other animals carry seeds far and wide on their fur. These

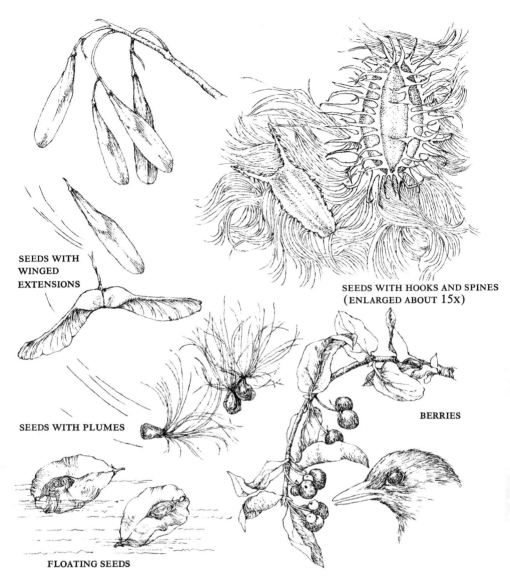

SEEDS WITH
WINGED
EXTENSIONS

SEEDS WITH HOOKS AND SPINES
(ENLARGED ABOUT 15X)

SEEDS WITH PLUMES

BERRIES

FLOATING SEEDS

seeds usually have sharp hooks or spines that stick to the hairs.

In all these ways plants and animals constantly keep moving to new ponds and lakes. When the conditions are suitable for them, they reproduce and increase in number.

Now let us return to the beginning of our story. A newly formed pond near Lake Michigan has a bare, sandy bottom. Many tiny algae live in the water, along with microscopic plants and animals called *plankton*. They provide food for the next larger animals of the pond, and these in turn provide food for still bigger ones.

Snails and mussels live on the sandy bottom of the pond. And here, too, are large-mouthed bass and jewel-like sunfish that make their nests on the sandy floor.

After some years a large, branching green alga, *Chara*, begins to grow and cover the bottom of the pond. Now fish that need hiding and nesting places in plants find protection.

Along with the bass and sunfish there are mud minnows and golden shiners. These fish place their eggs on the Chara instead of on the sandy bottom.

The Chara lives and grows and dies and adds its remains to the bottom of the pond. Other plants and animals in the pond die, and their remains decay and form a layer of *humus*—the name given to any decayed plant or animal matter. It is usually brown or black in color. So the pond bottom begins to be mucky instead of sandy, and this paves the way for other plants that require such a bottom. Slowly and gradually the vegetation in the pond changes.

Cattails, reeds, and bulrushes begin to grow at the edges of the pond. Their roots are in the soft, oozy muck at the bottom, and their stems are above the surface of the water. Where the water is from two to five feet deep, there are water lilies. Their roots are in the mud, but their shiny round leaves float on the surface. If you peer down into this pond farther in toward the center where the water is from five to ten feet deep, you will find the kinds of plants widely used in aquariums. Their stems and leaves are entirely under water.

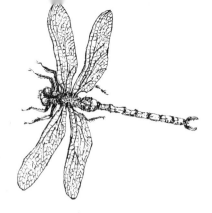

As the vegetation in the pond changes, the animal population changes too. The plants whose stems and leaves are above the water provide resting places for many new kinds of animals. Besides some gill-breathing snails that get their oxygen directly from the water, there are now many lung-breathing snails that climb to the surface on the plants to get fresh supplies of air.

Many kinds of insects climb around on the vegetation under the water. Some of these are the young stages of mayflies and dragonflies. When they are ready to change into adults, they climb up the stems into the air. Then their skins split open and the winged mayflies and dragonflies emerge and fly off. During this critical period in their lives these insects can live only where plants or rocks or logs provide a dry support.

While they are still in the water the young mayflies and dragonflies provide food for the crayfish, frogs, salamanders, turtles, and fish that live in the pond.

The fish are now mud species, like the black bullhead (a catfish).

COURTESY OF THE AMERICAN MUSEUM OF NATURAL HISTORY

The bottom of the pond keeps building up with the remains of dead plants and animals. It keeps getting muckier and more shallow. As time goes on there is less and less open water space in the center. Each zone of plants moves farther

in toward the center. The water lilies take root in the places once occupied only by submerged water plants. The cattails, reeds, bulrushes, and grasses now grow over the decaying remains of the water lilies.

The pond has gradually become a *marsh,* with only small areas of open water left between the advancing plants.

As the plants increase, the fish die and disappear because

U.S. FOREST SERVICE

the water is too muddy and shallow for them. Frogs, salamanders, and turtles remain and feed on the many insects
that live in or around the marsh plants.

Birds are busy feeding in and around the marsh. Some, such as ducks and other ducklike birds, the grebes and coots, swim and search for food in the open-water areas. Swamp sparrows feed on the seeds of the plants and so do the red-winged blackbirds, the dark birds that show flashes of red on their shoulders as they take off from their perches. Marsh wrens hang onto the stems and leaves of the reeds along the shore. These little brown birds are hard to see, but their voices ring over the marsh during the day and on moonlit nights. They find plenty of insect food on the plants around the edge of the marsh. Herons and bitterns wade in the shallow water and stab their sharp bills down after crayfish, frogs, or fish.

The marsh keeps filling. Soil washes in from the surrounding land, and the remains of plants and animals keep building up the bottom. What happens next depends upon where the marsh is. If it happens to be in a prairie region, the marsh gradually fills with grasses and becomes part of the prairie.

The story we are telling is of a marsh near forest land. After a long period of time a ring of bushes appears around

the edges of the marsh where once there were just cattails and bulrushes. Scattered in among the bushes are a few trees. Slowly and gradually the ring of bushes expands toward the center. More and more trees grow where before there were only a few. They form a circle around the outside of the bushes. These trees—ashes, elms, silver and red maples—are the kinds that can stand very wet soil.

If we could somehow speed up this very slowly changing scene and flash it on a screen, we would see the band of trees widen until it occupies the entire marsh. The marsh has become a *swamp forest.*

In the swamp forest you can find brightly colored wood ducks that make their nests in hollow trees. The woodcock is here too, but it is hard to find. Its brownish colors look like dead leaves, and when this bird settles in among the fallen leaves on the ground, it melts into the background.

Above in the trees the green heron has a platform of twigs that serves as its nest. Woodpeckers move into these woods as the trees get older. Bluejays, chickadees, and nuthatches come and find nesting places here.

The trees of the swamp forest grow taller and taller and cast more and more shade. They slowly but surely change conditions so much that their own offspring trees can no longer grow under their shade. New kinds of trees that can sprout and grow in soft, filtered light now take root.

The kinds of trees that grow depend upon where the swamp forest is. In the area around Lake Michigan right now you can find swamp forests that are slowly changing into another stage. Mixed in with the elms, ashes, and maples of the swamp forest there are white and red oaks, cherry trees, tulip trees, hickories, and sugar maples. We do not know yet exactly what will happen in this area, but we can predict that the forest of

mixed trees will become a beech and sugar-maple forest sometime in the distant future because there are beech and sugar-maple forests in the surrounding areas.

The wind brings the winged seeds of the sugar maples, and squirrels keep bringing in beechnuts from the surrounding country. These seeds can sprout and grow in very deep shade. Some sugar maples are already growing in the forest. More sugar maples and beech trees will take root and grow taller and taller until eventually they will replace the other trees.

Although we call the forest *beech-maple,* this does not mean that there are no other kinds of trees in such a forest. Often birch, linden, oak, and hemlock trees are mixed in with the beeches and maples. But beeches and maples are the most abundant trees in this forest.

Sugar maple, beech, hemlock forest

U.S. FOREST SERVICE

In a beech-maple forest the tall trees spread a heavy curtain of leaves over the ground below. There are hardly any open, sunny spaces. Only a fraction of the light above the forest filters through. The forest is damp, too. The dampness and shade suit salamanders and frogs. Earthworms, ants, crickets, millipedes, centipedes, snails, and slugs live in rotting logs

and under the carpet of dead leaves on the forest floor.

Thousands of insects get their food from the leaves and bark of the trees. Caterpillars munch leaf after leaf. Beetles chew bark and bore into wood. Plant lice suck the juices of the leaves. And a whole army of birds search all levels of the forest for these insects.

Some birds search the forest floor. The wood thrush pulls earthworms out of their tunnels underground. The ovenbird finds ants in rotting logs. Chickadees, nuthatches, and black and white warblers search the small trees in the lower levels of the forest. Scarlet tanagers search the upper layers in the taller trees and gulp down caterpillars. Here too are bluejays, vireos, woodpeckers, flycatchers, and many kinds of warblers.

Short-tailed shrews and white-footed mice are numerous. A scientist studying the animal life of the beech-maple forest found that he could catch one of these animals at every stump or log. Their tunnels and runways formed a network of passages under the litter of dead leaves.

Chipmunks, gray squirrels, and flying squirrels are abundant. They have a forest full of beechnuts and maple seeds to feed on. There are bigger animals here too—raccoons, gray foxes, and deer.

The beech-maple forest represents the final stage of the plant-succession story for this region. Young beech and maple trees can grow under the deep shade of tall beeches and maples. Because these dominant trees of the forest can re-

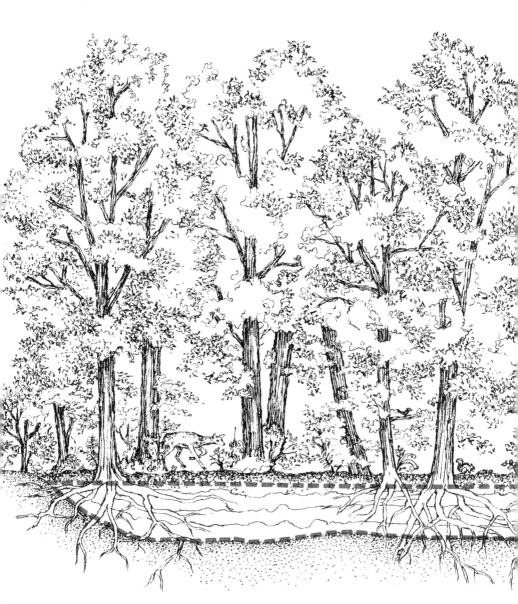

place themselves as the older trees die, the forest will stay in a "steady state" for a very long time and will not be replaced by another community of plants. Such a forest is called a *climax community*.

The story of filling ponds will have different endings depending upon where the ponds are. In different parts of the country there are different kinds of plants that represent the climax communities. It depends upon the climate. Certain trees grow best in the cold north—and so you will find pine, hemlock, spruce, and fir dominating the north woods.

U.S. FOREST SERVICE

U.S. FOREST SERVICE

The eastern half of the United States has extensive forests of beech-maple and oak-hickory.

COURTESY OF THE AMERICAN MUSEUM OF NATURAL HISTORY

In the Midwest, prairie grasses are the dominant vegetation.

In the warm areas along the coasts of the south Atlantic and Gulf states there are forests of long-leafed pine.

U.S. FOREST SERVICE

U.S. FOREST SERVICE

In the Rocky Mountains, great forests of pine, spruce, and fir cover the slopes.

U.S. FOREST SERVICE

Near the Pacific there are coastal forests of redwoods and others of fir, hemlock, cedar, and spruce.

Forest Regions of the United States

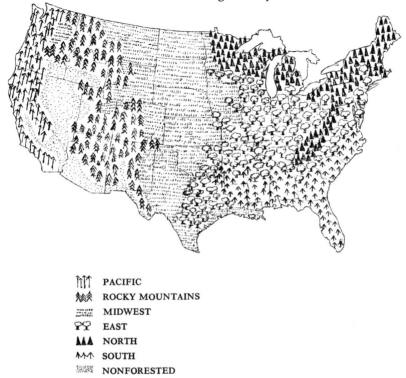

⋔⋔⋔	PACIFIC
𝌆𝌆	ROCKY MOUNTAINS
≈≈	MIDWEST
⋎⋎	EAST
▲▲▲	NORTH
∿∿	SOUTH
▒▒	NONFORESTED

    The basic story is the same. The water of the pond is gradually replaced by plant life. But the succession will always end with plant life typical of the stable plant communities of the region.

    Even stable plant communities do not always remain the same. They may be flooded. Or they may be destroyed by fire. Or there may be a landslide. If any such things happen, the plant communities will be destroyed and the area may become bare land again. In that case a whole new series of changes will start.

In most parts of the world bare land does not stay bare for long. Plants enter an area and slowly change the bare land until it is covered with vegetation again. When farmland was abandoned near Ann Arbor, Michigan, and a field was left bare, this is what happened:

Many plants appeared the first season after the field was abandoned. Some came from seeds left in the ground or carried there by wind or birds. Other plants came from underground parts that had stayed alive in the earth of the plowed field. Ragweed, prickly lettuce, Queen Anne's lace, and several kinds of grasses were abundant.

In a few years the field was covered with a dense mat of grasses. There were many other kinds of plants present too. Some of these were very slow growers and would not be

FARMLAND   TEN YEARS LATER

noticeable until later. If you had looked carefully among the grasses, you would have found small blackberry, raspberry, and other bushes, as well as a number of young trees. You would also have found many plants left over from the earlier stage.

As time went by asters and goldenrods became mixed with the grasses. Meanwhile the bushes and trees grew steadily. In the next years they grew bigger and bigger and cast more and more shade. They gradually made it impossible for the asters, goldenrods, and grasses to grow. Sumac, blackberry, and raspberry bushes became the most common plants. There were a number of elm, hawthorn, and black cherry trees scattered over the area.

TWENTY-FIVE YEARS LATER

The trees steadily increased in height and spread out until they overtopped and shaded the bushes. Twenty-five years from the time the field was abandoned, it was in a *tree stage* consisting largely of elms, black cherries, and hawthorns. All of these trees required considerable light. And their own seedling trees could not grow under their shade. But present under these trees were seedlings of oaks and hickories that could grow in their shade.

The study went only this far, but from what we know, we can predict that slowly and gradually the pioneer trees will be replaced by oaks and hickories. Since there are beech and maple forests in the area, seedling beeches and maples will begin to grow in the shade of the oaks and hickories. Once the beeches and maples grow tall, they will cast so much shade that young oaks and hickories will no longer be able to grow. Gradually these trees will disappear, and the forest will change to beech-maple.

This is only an example of what happens to a particular piece of bare land in the state of Michigan. But wherever bare land occurs (unless it is in Antarctica or high on top of a mountain), there is a gradual succession of plant communities until a stage is reached that is representative of the stable plant community of the region.

Look around you to find places where ponds are filling in or where bushes and trees are showing in abandoned fields. Around a pond you can sometimes find zones of vegetation

U.S. FOREST SERVICE

that mirror the stages a pond goes through as it fills. If you find such a place, get into a boat and go to the center of the pond. You are in the region of deep, open water. Now move into shallower water and peer down to see the submerged water plants. In still shallower water you will hit the water-lily zone. Then comes the marshy zone where cattails and rushes grow. Beyond this are bushes and behind the bushes you may see trees. If you just imagine these zones moving in to the center of the pond, you will have the story of pond to forest before you.

If you see an abandoned field in which young seedling trees are growing, you know now that it will not be too long before the trees will overtop the other vegetation.

The landscape looks quiet and still, but something is happening all the time. The world of nature is always changing.

U.S. FOREST SERVICE

3927900207110 DLIFLC
Chamberlin Library

J 581 SELS 1964   c.1
Selsam, Millicent Ellis

Birth of a forest
5may87

Chamberlin Library
Building 4275
Fort Ord, CA 93941-5605